Gospel Entrepreneur

A Guide to Starting a
Kingdom Business

Michael R Baer

Introduction

Over the years, I've written a lot about Kingdom Business—why we do it, how it's related to the Gospel, strategic applications and so forth. I've also taught many entrepreneurs how to do it. But I've never written down how to do it in a simple book form. That is the purpose of *Gospel Entrepreneur.* It is a short, ready to apply, "how to" sort of book.

My associates and I have been blessed by God to help start literally hundreds of businesses around the world. Some have failed. Most have succeeded. And all have been built upon and built for the discipling of the nations.

My hope is that you will join those who have sensed the call of God to start a business for His glory, to align it with His global purpose, and to experience great joy in creating an enterprise of your very own.

Chapter 1

What is a Kingdom Business? Why start a Kingdom Business?

Over the past 25 years, I have had the privilege to work with a wonderful network of brothers and sisters in the Business as Mission movement. For a major part of that time, I worked with the Jholdas Project--a small business incubator focused on establishing persecuted believers in business so they can support their families, their struggling local churches and, ultimately, indigenous mission work. To date, we have seen over 1300 businesses started and approximately 500 churches planted as a result--primarily among the unreached people groups of the world. Along the way, we have learned a few things about starting a Kingdom Business that I will share with you in the following chapters.

Definitions

What exactly are we talking about? Business as

Mission (BAM) is the natural extension of my commitment to Christ in the sphere of life to which He has called me. It may be in my home country or it may be in another country. The simple reality is that business is a fully legitimate calling from God and the disciple is meant to enter into that calling with headlong, joyful abandon and focus on living for Jesus in that context.

However, there is another vital dimension to BAM. My career or my business or my startup needs to be deliberately, thoughtfully connected to God's purpose in the world. In my opinion, it is this characteristic that is the *sine qua non* (absolutely essential) of Business as Mission. A quick survey of Scripture will lead you to conclude that God was, is and always will be focused on filling up this earth with people who know, honor and love Him. So the question comes: how is my business intentionally connected to that?

And, finally, a Kingdom Business is one that seeks to operate on principles and values drawn from and consistent with the revelation of God's Word. There is far more in Scripture about work and the marketplace than we have ever imagined. We must learn to dig it out and apply it fearlessly in

our companies for the glory of God.
Motivations

Simon Sinek recently published a book entitled *Start with Why*. It's an excellent read and there is also a TedTalk on the subject entitled *The Golden Circle*. It's all about core motivations, reasons for action, and motivations. In the same way, the Kingdom Entrepreneur needs to think through the "why" of his or her business early in the launch process.

The late management guru, Peter Drucker, once said, "The purpose of all business is to make a profit." I wholeheartedly agree and so does Scripture. As an institution of God (see Genesis 1), enterprise is purposed with creating the wealth necessary for the other institutions of society to function. Thus, no profit means no business; it doesn't matter what you call it.

However, like every other institution, business has multiple levels of its core purpose. To create wealth, yes. To make a profit, yes. But there are many dimensions of wealth and profit beyond today's fallen definition of "money only" or "shareholder value." There is the benefit brought to a family, a community, or a nation through business done God's way. There is an environmental responsibility borne by all humans and all businesses based upon the Creation Mandate:

> Then God said, Let us make man in our image, after our likeness. And let them have dominion over the fish of the sea and over the birds of the heavens and over the livestock and over all the earth and over every creeping thing that creeps on the earth. So God created man in his own image, in the image of God he created him; male and female he created them. And God blessed them. And God said to them, Be fruitful and multiply and fill the earth and subdue it and have dominion over the fish of the sea and over the birds of the heavens and over every living thing that moves on the earth. And God said, Behold, I have given you every plant yielding seed that is on the face of all the earth, and every tree with seed in its fruit. You shall have them for food. And to every beast of the earth and to every bird of the heavens and to everything that creeps on the earth, everything that has the breath of life, I have given every green

plant for food. And it was so. And God saw everything that he had made, and behold, it was very good. And there was evening and there was morning, the sixth day. (Genesis 1:26-31, ESV)

And, most importantly, there is the doxological "why." All things are designed and created for the glory and worship of God. (1 Corinthians 10:31) Business is no exception.

Conclusion

So the starting point for Kingdom Business startups is the "what" and the "why." We must be clear on these points or we shall forever be looking over our shoulders and living in "semi-apology" for our business and its success.

Chapter 2

6 Questions to Answer Before Starting

If you are serious about starting a business or being part of a startup business that is committed to being what God intended business to be--real, for profit, connected to His purposes--then there are several key questions for you to consider prior to going very far into the process.

What is your role going to be?

That may seem like begging the question. Of course, I am going to be an entrepreneur. Strike that. THE entrepreneur. Perhaps. But it may be that God is calling you to be a part of a startup rather than the "starter upper." In that case, you need to determine if you are an entrepreneur (about 15% of the world's population leans this way), a professional manager (e.g. a finance guy, an operations guy, a marketing guy, etc.), an employee (non-management such as technical or production), a consulting resource or an investor/lender.

Where are you going to locate your business?

This is your Acts 1:8 question. Are you going to start/expand in your Jerusalem (domestic), Judea and Samaria (simple cross cultural) or in the uttermost corners of the earth (unreached people groups and restricted access countries)? Your answer will determine many of the more detailed steps you'll be taking.

What size will you be?

I know. The answer is "as big as God wants." However, having some sense of determination of the size of your company will affect your funding strategy, your staffing strategy, your marketing strategy...you get the point. So will you work in the micro-enterprise space (MED)? This usually entails very low startup costs (less than $5,000 USD) and a very small workforce (usually family and a very few more). Will you pursue small to mid-sized enterprise (SME)? Startup costs are higher and can range from $15,000 to $100,000 USD; this type of business is rarely able to be launched by 1 person and will require a team in the very beginning. Or are you pursuing a large, overseas private equity company (OPE)? Now we are talking big dollars for equipment, machinery, inventory, staff, legal compliance and so on. One other option is multinational expansion (CCE)--you have a sustainable business at home and you are going to expand cross culturally.

What is your purpose?

This is a sticker wicket than you might think and depending on how many people you have involved and what kind of financial investors you have this question may make or break your startup. Here are a few purposes (other than the given of gaining and keeping customers and making a profit): equipping nationals, funding nationals and national ministries, entry to closed countries (by which I *do not mean* "business as visa"), engaging nationals in the marketplace and/or the government, employing nationals, or general community development.

Where is your funding coming from?

Everyone has an opinion on this, so I will go ahead and give you mine. Sooner or later if your business does not self-fund (and by that I mean leaving donations behind), then it is not really a business. So here are some options to consider. There is temporary donation to self-sustainability; in this the startup capital is in the form of contributions with a definite timetable by which they will end. It is venture capital with no expectation of return. There is self-funding (the most common method worldwide). This can be personal savings, liquidation of assets, friends and family, credit cards, etc. Some call this the "bet the farm" approach. An increasing number of BAM companies are starting with investor funding; just like any other business, investors support the idea, the entrepreneur, the strategy and put their money in. How they get their money out is negotiable. To some it's a loan with repayment at interest; to others it's stock ownership. Each method has pros and cons. We will discuss this further in a later chapter.

What is your Kingdom Impact Strategy?

In every business we have started or funded around the world, we have required a clear statement of how the founder and/or management team intends to bring glory to God and engage in discipling the nations. We call this a Kingdom Impact Statement. We've seen amazingly creative ideas over the years usually arranged along the following lines. Employing believers to create economic traction for the local Christian community. Employing unbelievers as a discipleship opportunity. Utilizing disciple makers in key company roles like HR, finance, etc. Engaging customers and vendors in order to display and communicate the Gospel. Bringing social change to the local community as in rescuing victims of human trafficking or fighting government corruption. And, as you can imagine, every conceivable combination of the above is going on out there as well. The key is to know what your purpose is.

Conclusion

Working through these questions takes time and is well worth the effort. I encourage you to prayerfully go through them. Take your time. Seek godly counsel. A solid foundation is more likely to lead to a solid business in the future

Chapter 3

What's the Big Idea?

Your idea...your concept is critical to your startup. It may seem like a statement of the blindingly obvious, but I will risk making it anyway. To start a business you have to have an idea: what are you going to do to bring a valuable product or service to those who need or want it? You'd be amazed at how many people I speak with who want to start a business, but when asked what kind of business, what product or service they will offer, they don't have a clue!

What Kinds of Ideas are There?

Of course there are good ideas and bad ideas. We'll explore that in a later chapter. What I mean here by "kinds of ideas" is the approach or angle we take to the market. What position will we stake out?

For example, there are business ideas that are

about innovation, i.e. creating something that's never been done before or combining things in a way they've never been combined before. Steve Jobs is a prime example of this kind of idea. There are ideas that are about price--using a new technology or delivery mechanism or manufacturing technique that enables you to bring your product to market cheaper than anyone else and still maintain strong margins There are ideas that are about quality and service. You will do it better, faster, and friendlier than anyone else; who would have thought that an online shoe store would be wildly successful--the guys at Zappos!

Where Does it Come From?

While every now and then I hear stories about business ideas that came on the mountain top much like the 10 Commandments, most ideas or business concepts come to us in much more mundane ways and from mundane sources. If you are sensing a call to launch a Kingdom Business here are a few suggested "places" where you may find a good idea; my only caution is that you begin and end your quest in prayer for He is ultimately the source of all good ideas.

First, start with what needs or gaps do you see in the marketplace? What do people need or want that they are either not getting or not getting in a way they like, that works or that they can afford? Second, read good books of all kinds. Business books. Christian books. Novels. History. Biographies. Science. Anything. Stimulate your mind with something besides TV or social media. Third, look around at what others are doing. You may get the idea to do what they are doing or do it better or even do the exact opposite. Fourth, explore franchise opportunities. Some will say that franchises are not entrepreneurial. Nothing could be further from the truth. There are all kinds of ideas that are being franchised around the world.

Another approach that is embarrassingly simple is called the 'Three Legged Stool.' What is your background? What are you good at? What do you have a passion for? Navigating these questions often may enable you to locate your idea.

How Can You Explain It?

Assuming that you have an idea, I would ask you the third key question: can you explain it in a way that others understand and embrace? I don't mean sell your product; I mean explain your idea. If it leaves people stupefied or confused, it may make you feel smart, but it won't work in the business world. I use this rule of thumb: if it won't fit on 1 sheet of paper or can't be sketched on a napkin, go back to the drawing board. Simplicity, not complicatedness, is what you need.

Conclusion

Everything else discussed in this book flows out of having your idea in place. It doesn't have to be complete and most likely it won't be. But having the idea is the seed from which your startup will grow. No idea...no business. Bad idea...bad business.

Chapter 4

The "Voice of the Bazaar"

When we first started our business incubation work in Central Asia in the 1990's, we had to quickly introduce local entrepreneurs to the idea of a market study. How would they know if their idea was a good one? How would they know who their competition was, how much to charge, etc.? When we first began to talk about the "voice of the market" they quickly translated that into the "voice of the bazaar." Not a bad translation all things considered. We created a list of 41 questions, called "The 41 Questions," that our students could go and answer in the bazaar. I suggest that every entrepreneur needs to create their own set of questions to answer before they launch their business. Here are a few to consider:

Who do you think will buy your product or service?

One young brother came to us with the idea for

custom leather Bible covers. In Kyrgyzstan. In 1998. I asked him gently how many believers he thought were in his country. He said maybe 1000. I asked how many owned Bibles. Maybe 100. How many of those could afford to buy a leather cover? Maybe 10. I think you see the point.

Who else is offering a similar product or service?

Sometimes the answer is no one. Great...but why? It's more likely that you are one of several or even many in your space. Who are the others? What do you know about them? In WWII, posters encouraged the Allies to "Know Your Enemy!" We need to know our competition.

How much are people paying for this product or service if it's available? How much will they pay if it's not?

How do you know how much to charge? Do you start with your costs and add your profit margin? Or do you start with what the customers are willing to pay and work backward, i.e. control your cost to create profit? Price points can make or break any company, but especially a startup.

In what way is your product or service different than what competitors are offering?

I remember one candidate in Asia was going to start an egg business. He would collect eggs from farmers and sell them for the farmers in the bazaar. One of our faculty pressed him repeatedly on how he would differentiate and get attention from potential buyers. He seemed quite frustrated by the line of questioning and finally blurted out, "I will hang a sign out that says "I have EGGS!" That was enough. He was the only one selling eggs in the bazaar.

Where and how are your competitors operating?

Location is essential to certain types of businesses. To others, it's irrelevant. Is the product or service delivered in person or virtually, in a store or online?

Conclusion

Starting a business without studying the market is a formula for disaster. Unless you are Steve Jobs and can create entire industries from nothing, the time you spend to understand the environment into which you are entering is to roll the dice--and they often come up snake eyes.

Chapter 5

5 Key Components of a Business Plan

So you have to have a business plan. Sorry, but that's the way it is. And there are at least three reasons to put the time and effort into building this out. First, nothing will help you clarify your idea and viability than a business plan. Second, it is one of the best ways to help you think around corners and face issues we all tend to overlook in our dreaming and scheming stage. Third, no business plan means no investors.

A Resource to Help

There are plenty of paid business plan apps that you can find online. You can also pay a consultant to help you write your plan (or, worse, even write it for you). I suggest the cheap and personal route.

The Key Components

You can make a b-plan simple, smart or extremely

over-engineered. It's up to you and determined primarily by your purpose for writing it in the first place. Nevertheless, here are most if not all of the key pieces you need to work through:

> *Executive Summary*--this "less than a page" explanation of your business should be written last even though it will appear first.
>
> *Concept*--this section can run from one to several pages depending on your particular business. In it you will outline your basic concept, your product or service and how you plan on delivering it to market. If this is not clear then the rest of the b-plan (whether it is for you or for investors) will be fuzzy.
>
> *Market Data*--what did you learn in your market research? This is where you explain that there are people who want or need your product, who are willing to pay for it, where they are, how you're going to reach them, how much you are going to charge, how many there are, etc. This is where you will also explain who your competition is and what you've learned about them and, most importantly, how your product or service is

different, better, cheaper, faster, etc. In other words, how will you win?

Startup Plan--there are many steps required in actually getting a business up and running. These activities range from incorporation to recruiting your team to choosing a name to you name it. These need to be in a timeline format that demonstrates you know what needs to be done and when you plan on having each item accomplished.

Financials--you might think that this is all you really need and that investors/lenders will look here first. Only the inexperienced ones. Having been involved in over 1000 small startups and several multi-hundred-million dollar deals I can assure you that investors want the financials, but they also want the story. Your financials are essentially 3 sets of projections: best case, worst case, and expected case. They are typically done on a spreadsheet. They will include revenue projections per month for at least 3 years, costs of sales/goods, operating expenses, anticipated profits and losses, and cumulative cash flow to show when the enterprise will actually start generating positive cash.

Conclusion

These components are true for every business plan--some more some less. But what about the Kingdom? I'll address this in the next chapter.

Chapter 6

Your Business. God's Mission.

Business as Mission (BAM) is based on the "seamless integration of business as mission." In other words, there is no distinction between the realms of business and God's purposes in the world. To help keep that reality in focus, I advocate integrating Kingdom Thinking into the business planning process. It's not a separate step (although it's a separate blog) and flows quite nicely into the plan.

Kingdom Impact Statement

Where most business plans have some kind of Mission Statement (not to be confused with a trite slogan or bumper sticker jingle). A true mission statement tells what you do, why you do it, who you do it, and how you do it. A Kingdom Impact Statement (KIS) is the same thing--except that it involves the dimension of God's purpose in the world. By way of example, the KIS of one of my companies reads: *The Jholdas Group exists to support church planting among the unreached peoples of the 10/40 Window through the seamless integration of business as mission.*

Intentional Connection to God's Mission

I deliberately use the singular of "mission" to distinguish it from your church's "missions program." God is at work (and always has been) to restore all things affected by the fall to His own glory. My connection to that is imperative as a disciple of Christ. So, how is my business connected? While this may be a moving or evolving target based on our understanding, the more I can articulate it the better. Here are some questions to consider:

1. Will I operate at home or abroad or both?
2. Will I hire believers?
3. Will I hire and disciple unbelievers?
4. Will I place disciplemakers in key positions?
5. Will I equip nationals to start their own businesses, distributorships, etc.?
6. Will I sell to nationals or internationals?

Kingdom Objectives

In all plans there are financial objectives, market objectives, profit objectives, geographical objectives. What about Kingdom Objectives? What will the measurable outcomes be in and through your business that are overtly related to the Great Commission--in its fullest application of individual salvation all the way to societal transformation.

One business I know of was started to provide jobs for reclaimed prostitutes in Calcutta. The metrics are more than just how much money was made. They include how many of them come out of prostitution, how many are employed, how many remain free, etc.

Utilization of Profit

Profit is not a dirty word. In fact, you will often hear me say, "No profit, no business!" However, as Kingdom People we do need to be thoughtful about the way we use the profits of our business. Providing well for yourself and your family is totally legitimate, and I'd urge you to beware of those who think they have the right to judge what that means for you. What other uses of the proceeds of the business will there be? Reinvestment?

Expansion? Giving? Community service?

Conclusion

By taking these components and those outlined in the previous chapter, you have a pretty good shot at developing a well thought out Kingdom Business Plan. Next, we'll discuss your team and your funding. Both are critical

Chapter 7

4 Hiring Warnings and 5 Key Positions in Your Start-up

I've consulted with a lot of business startups-- usually after they've stalled or run into trouble. The problem in almost every case I have seen is not funding. It's people. Not having the right people around you from Day One is Problem One. This chapter and the next will address some of the key things to think about when it comes to your team.

Warnings

I don't want to dwell on the negative, but there are some simple warnings I want to share that may save you some heartache down the road:

> *Never Settle.* There is something about Christians that compels us to settle for less than excellence. Not only is this counter to Scripture, but it's also counter to your success. A substandard employee is just

that--substandard. And their work will be substandard as well.

Beware of the "Buds." The most common thing I've seen in new businesses, Kingdom or otherwise, is what I call "the Frat boys." Hiring friends, family, and church colleagues is easy. However, if you don't apply a rigorous selection process and somehow give them a "pass" it is you who will pay the price. Friendship is great, but it won't sell anything or produce a clean financial report.

Don't be Cheap. Since this business is for the Lord your employees shouldn't expect a market-competitive income should they? Right? WRONG! Sooner or later the underpaid employee will end up quitting or "quitting and staying." If profit is a worthy motive for business (and it is), then so is the desire on the part of your team to make a good living.

Avoid the Hurry. "Hire in haste; repent in leisure." It is a lot easier to hire someone than it is to get rid of them. Whether you're dealing with the highly litigious North

American HR context or the problem of letting an expat go in a foreign country or the cultural issues of firing a national, it's all bad. Take your time. Know what you want and need. Then find it.

Composition

Exactly what you need in term of skills depends largely on the type of business you are starting and the particular impact strategy you've chosen. Nevertheless, here are some basic positions you need to have filled--even if you have the same person filling two boxes on the org chart or if you outsource.

> *Finance and Accounting:* It's not just about reports. It's about regulations, tax compliance, and information. Here's a tip: businesses don't fail for lack of profit; they fail for lack of cash. Think about that. A finance guy knows what I'm saying. If you don't, then you need to hire one.
>
> *Operations:* Whatever your product or service, someone has to run the day-to-day operations. Planning. Making. Stocking.

Shipping. Delivering. Inspecting. Improving. Supply chain. Transportation. A lot goes into running a business.

Information Technology: Even if you're not a technology company (and the odds are you will be), there's a ton of technology you have to be on top of. Networks. Systems. Hardware. Software. Websites. Lions, tigers and bears...oh my!

Business Development: Know sales or have no sales. Products and services don't sell themselves. The market doesn't just wake up one day and go to your site. Someone needs to wake up every day thinking about how to let people know what you've got, why it's better than whatever your competition is offering, how to convince them to buy from you and how to keep them buying. Call it sales or marketing or BD or whatever. Just do it!

Human Resources: The legal environment when it comes to employing people is thornier than ever. It's toxic with government over-regulation, lawsuits, and more. In some countries you can even wind up in jail for violating some obscure "human resource" regulation. Get someone who can keep up with the laws and the trends and who is forceful enough to keep you out of trouble.

Conclusion

Your team is your future. It's that simple. Build a good one. In the next chapter, we'll examine the qualifications of Kingdom professionals and unbelievers as well as when and how to outsource some of your team functions.

Chapter 8

2 Temptations of Staffing Your Start-up

The greatest business idea in the world with sub-standard employees will probably fail. This is at least equally true if not more so for a Kingdom Business. In the last chapter, we looked at the dangers in hiring or building your team for a startup. This post will deal with two temptations.

Qualifications

Let's assume for the sake of argument that your candidates have the technical qualifications to do their jobs--they know accounting, they're experienced in technology, they've actually operated something prior to this venture, etc. Just because you are launching your business to glorify God does not mean that you can take someone who knows nothing about finance and make him your Controller or a novice in the sales process and declare him to be Chief Marketing Officer. And, if you're one of those magical thinkers that will point out how God calls and uses the weak, then we are not going to agree very much in this area. With only an extremely small number of notable exceptions, having the basics to actually *do the job* are a prerequisite for joining my team.

But there are other qualifications that matter as much as technical ability. Character. Spiritual maturity. Flexibility. Humility. Passion for the lost. Deep honesty. Cross cultural giftings. Supporting spouse.

Some of the qualifications depend on your staff strategy--will you hire only Christians or will you hire unbelievers? Are you international? In a least-reached area? Major western city?

Here's the point: if you compromise on technical ability then important technical things like tax compliance will likely suffer; if you compromise on character (even if you are hiring unbelievers) your entire company culture will suffer.

"Wow!" you say. "This is hard!" Yep.

Outsourcing

For any startup, I would say that you should outsource everything and every role you possibly can. Period. Hold to the qualifications outlined above. And use a staffing company, your CPA, a consulting firm, a freelancer, an intern, a payroll service. The fewer people you hire on the less fixed cost you have and the more flexibility you gain. Besides, you may be able to get all the accounting or IT expertise you need in about 12 hours a month--a lot cheaper than a full time financial or technology guy.

But can you do this for a Kingdom Company in another country? Sure. It's no different. Maybe more difficult and maybe more complicated, but still a good move.

Conclusion

The two temptations I've seen entrepreneurs fall into are investing way to much in the trappings of business (nice office, great computers, etc.) and hiring less than qualified employees too soon. Follow the advice of this chapter and the previous one and increase your chances of success.

Chapter 9

5 Funding Models for Your Kingdom Start-up

The still famous line from the movie *Jerry McGuire* is "Show me the money!" Some of you have been thinking that as you've read the previous 8 chapters in this book. How do I get money to launch my startup? I'm going to outline several models you can consider:

The "Missionary for a Moment" Model

I have to tell you upfront that I have rejected this model for years. However, recently a close brother whom I respect greatly challenged my thinking and got me a little closer to acceptance than I was before.

The Momentary Missionary Model essentially uses raised donations or support to cover living, travel and certain startup expenses just like a normal missionary would raise support to cover living, travel and ministry expenses. What makes this work is that you are committing to your "donor-investors" to be off their giving roles within a specified period of time, to have your business profitable and to live off it.

Your donor audience in this scenario is sympathetic although they may not be the most investment savvy. Be careful to not take unintentional advantage of that sympathy. This is business.

The "What's Your Day Job" Model

The majority of small businesses start this way-- sometimes coupled with the next model. In this model, you and/or your spouse have a normal "day job" that you live off of while you are in the process of planning, launching and self-funding your new Kingdom Business.

The great advantage of this approach is that you aren't "betting the farm." The great disadvantage is that you aren't "betting the farm." You run the risk of ending up with a struggling "hobby" business instead of a real one and never finding the courage to go ahead and jump in with both feet.

The "Bootstrap" Model

If you read enough back issues of <u>Inc.</u> or <u>Entrepreneur</u> you will repeatedly come across the guy who exhausted his savings, maxed out his credit cards, and mortgaged his house to find enough money to launch a business and keep it afloat until the economic engine could kick in.

This is the riskiest of all methods but, in some ways, also the most rewarding. You make it or you don't. You win or you lose. And only you are left holding the bag. One of my BAM heroes started his company in China with $14,000 to his name; it went on to be a smash success.

The "Friends and Family" Plan

Mobile phone companies are not the only ones who can use this term. Plenty of entrepreneurs have started the same way. They may choose to invest (for equity), donate the money (not a bad way for Mom and Dad to share their inheritance with you tax free while they are still alive), or make a series of loans.

I think this is the easiest way to raise money (and

we probably aren't talking millions!). It's also fraught with some real problems--do they want a level of control? Will they be injecting their advice? What happens when you owe friends and family money? What happens if the business fails and you still owe your friends and family money?

The Angel or Venture Capital Model

To date, there are very few capital funds willing to invest in Kingdom Business outside of the Western world. If you are launching a company in Toronto or Terra Haute that is one thing and you may find funding for equity (and control) relatively easily. However, funding of this type where the investor expects a return on his or her investment is extremely hard to come by for opening a company in Bandung or Beijing. The risks are huge and there are virtually no track records of success; these two factors make true investors very nervous.

Conclusion

If you're thinking this is hard, then you are right. It is. However, at the same time don't forget that God is able to provide abundantly for any work that is of His initiation and for His exaltation. After all, the "cattle on a thousand hills are" His--He may just decide to sell a few and send the money to you!

About the Author

Michael R Baer

Michael Baer has over 25 years of experience in executive, organizational and leadership development. He is the founder of several businesses including a strategic consulting and business advisory firm, a construction company, and a bed and breakfast inn. Mike also serves as Executive Director of an international mission organization specializing in microenterprise and in this role he has launched a small business incubation process which is in use in over 27 countries.

As well as his rich experience in the business as mission (BAM) movement, Mike brings an understanding of the biblical basis for business that rejects the compartmentalizing of 'sacred-secular' thinking and presents an exciting perspective on the role of business in the Kingdom of God.

Other Books by Michael R Baer

Business as Mission

2IC: Business as Mission When You Aren't the Boss

Street Level Romans

Devotions for My Grandkids

Prayers for My Grandkids

www.ingramcontent.com/pod-product-compliance
Lightning Source LLC
Chambersburg PA
CBHW070408190526
45169CB00003B/1159